The Plans I Have For You

DEVOTIONAL

The Plans I Have For You

DEVOTIONAL

AMY PARKER

ILLUSTRATED BY
**VANESSA
BRANTLEY-NEWTON**

 ZONDERkidz™

ZONDERKIDZ

The Plans I Have for You Devotional
Copyright © 2015 by Amy Parker
Illustrations © 2015 by Vanessa Brantley-Newton

This title is also available as a Zondervan ebook.
Visit www.zondervan.com/ebooks

Requests for information should be addressed to:

Zonderkidz, 3900 *Sparks Dr. SE*, Grand Rapids, Michigan 49546

ISBN 978-0-310-72522-0

Art direction and design: Kris Nelson

Printed in China

15 16 17 18 19 /DHC/ 10 9 8 7 6 5 4 3 2 1

To Grandmommy and Granddaddy,
for your shining example of
living a life truly devoted to God
and for never doubting the
plans God had for me.
—AP

Teach them the way
that they should go.
For Sharonda Singelton and family.
—VBN

Sector 1: I've Got Big Plans for YOU! 13

Sector 2: I've Given YOU a Purpose........ 37

Sector 3: I Don't Do Things Small 59

Sector 6: What I Created YOU To Do 133

Hey, YOU!

Did you know that God wants to spend time with you? YES, YOU!

He wants to hear about your day, what you love, what gets on your nerves. Of course, he knows these things before you even think them— he really just wants to hear them from YOU. That's what a devotional is: a tool that helps you spend time with God and get to know him better by thinking about him, talking to him, and hearing from his Word.

These devotionals focus on God's plans for you, how to find your unique purpose in this world, and how to pursue that purpose with God's guidance. When you're a kid (even when you're an adult), it's sometimes hard to see your purpose in this big ol' world. But there's no doubt that God had a purpose for you before you were even born. He's given you a part in his plan—for the benefit of the world and your own life.

In order to learn about God's plans, you've got to spend time with him. Each day, try to find a quiet spot and read one devotional. Pray before or after or both! You can flip to a random page or read them in order. Look up the verses in your own Bible or just read them out of the book. But the one, single, solitary, absolute, most important thing is this: Spend time talking to and listening to God. Every day.

You don't even need this book to do that—but I hope it helps. And I also hope that it helps to paint a great big arrow pointing you down the path that God has waiting just for you.

I'm praying for you—and for the plans God has for YOU.

Love, Amy
♡

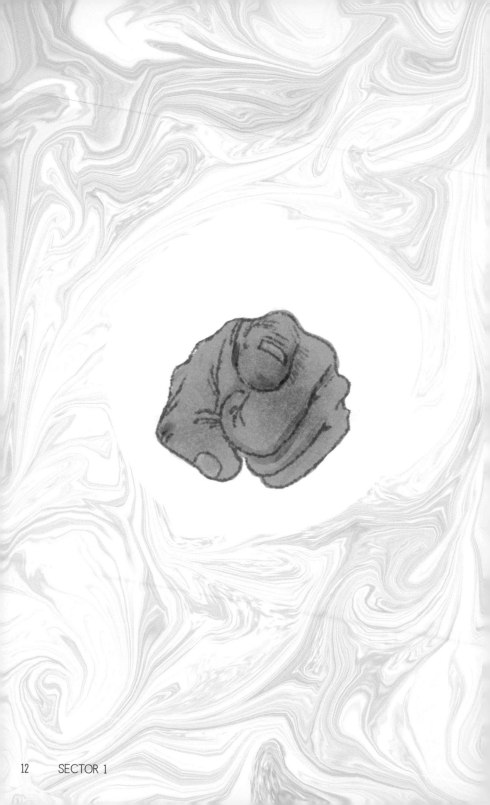

I've Got Big Plans for YOU!

Hey, YOU

I've got big plans for you!
Yes, YOU, and you,
and YOU over there too!

What plans do you feel God whispering to your heart?
In what ways have you seen others follow God's plans?

In the days that follow, we're going to explore the plans
God has for YOU...

I've Got Big Plans for Moses!

But when [Moses' mom] could
hide him no longer, she got a papyrus
basket for him and coated it with tar and pitch.
Then she placed the child in it and put it
among the reeds along the bank of the Nile.
His sister stood at a distance to
see what would happen to him.

EXODUS 2:3–4

Imagine how difficult it must have been for Moses' mother to put her tiny baby boy in a basket and send it down a river. Imagine how frightened Moses would have been—even as a baby—to see his mom getting farther and farther away as he entered strange surroundings. Imagine how his big sister, Miriam, felt as she watched her baby brother float away into the unknown.

But do you know who wasn't worried? God.

Imagine God smiling as Moses' mother carefully crafted the basket, as Moses wriggled in fear, as Miriam watched wide-eyed. God knew exactly what he had planned for Moses. And God knew it would take some stepping out in faith for Moses to get there.

If things seem a little scary for you right now,
if God's plans seem unclear, talk to him, trust him.
Just as he did for Moses,
God has big plans for YOU.

Trust in the Lord.

Do you ever feel like everything is out of whack? Like you're heading in the wrong direction? God knew there would be days like this.

Trust in the Lord with all your heart
and lean not on your own understanding;
in all your ways submit to him,
and he will make your
paths straight.

PROVERBS 3:5–6

Give God your questions,

your concerns, your heart.

He will guide you.

He Is Watching

He will not let your foot slip—
he who watches over you will not slumber.

PSALM 121:3

God never sleeps.
He watches over you day and night.
When you're frightened, worried, or feeling lonely,
he's there, waiting for you to whisper his name.

He Is Near

The LORD is near to all who call on him,
to all who call on him in truth.

PSALM 145:18

Feeling lonely?

Feeling blue?

Give God a call!

He's right there with

YOU.

He Directs

This is what the LORD says—
your Redeemer, the Holy One of Israel:
"I am the LORD your God, who teaches
you what is best for you, who directs
you in the way you should go."

ISAIAH 48:17

The God who told Noah to build an ark,
The One who parted the Red Sea,
The God who calmed the wind and waves—
That God directs you and me.

23

The Humble Hear

Only the humble will hear God's direction.

Prideful hearts won't need help.

The arrogant already know the way.

The haughty have their own things to do,

thankyouverymuch.

But those who admit they need God's guidance,

those who wait for instruction,

those who make time to listen ...

They will hear, and they will find the way.

ONLY THE HUMBLE WILL HEAR GOD'S DIRECTION

He guides the humble in what is right
and teaches them his way.

PSALM 25:9

Choose

**"Choose for yourselves this day whom you will serve . . .
But as for me and my household, we will serve the LORD."**

JOSHUA 24:15

God had big plans for Joshua. He had big plans for the Israelites too. But before they could fulfill God's plans, a choice had to be made. Would the Israelites serve the gods of the people around them? Or would they choose the one true God, the God who had guided them and provided for them throughout their journey? Joshua knew they could not serve both.

Joshua left the decision up to the Israelites, but he also made it very clear: he was choosing God.

Whom will you serve? Whom will you follow?
Whom do you choose?

Hope Fully

For in this hope we were saved.
But hope that is seen is no hope at all.
Who hopes for what they already have?
But if we hope for what we do not yet have,
we wait for it patiently.

ROMANS 8:24–25

Hope fully.

Wait patiently.

Dream big.

Look at all of the hope in these verses! But what does it all mean? Read through the verses again, carefully, slowly, phrase by phrase, and consider what God is trying to tell you about hope and the plans he has for YOU.

The Desires of Your Heart

**Take delight in the LORD,
and he will give you the desires of your heart.**

PSALM 37:4

What does your heart desire? To be rich and famous? To sail the seas? To eat a big piece of chocolate cake? Sooo, according to Psalm 37:4, if you delight in the Lord, he'll give you a big piece of chocolate cake! Right?

Well, not exactly.

As you learn more about God, you will find the true joy that comes with knowing him. You'll also see that what you really want begins to change. You may start to care a lot less about what you get and a lot more about what you give. God's desires become your desires. His plans become your plans. And your life will be better because of it.

Today, tell God the desires of your heart
and take delight in knowing that he will lead the way.

Step by Step

**In their hearts humans plan their course,
but the LORD establishes their steps.**

PROVERBS 16:9

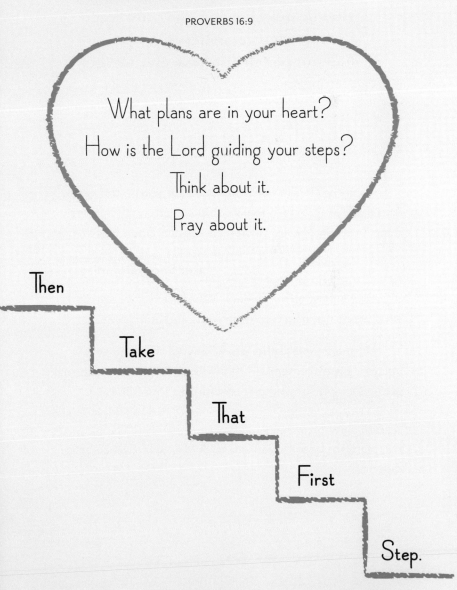

What plans are in your heart?

How is the Lord guiding your steps?

Think about it.

Pray about it.

Then

Take

That

First

Step.

The Biggest Plan

For God so loved the world
that he gave his one and only Son,
that whoever believes in him
shall not perish but have eternal life.

JOHN 3:16

You may not be sure of God's plans for you on this earth. And that's okay. In fact, that's completely normal. But one thing is certain: We are all offered a part in God's biggest plan.

God's biggest plan must include a humongous to-do list, right? Nope. Jesus has already done the hard part, leaving us just one thing to do: believe. When we do, we are offered what we do not deserve: forgiveness and eternal life.

Although God's other plans for your life may seem unclear, always remember that the biggest plan—the eternal plan—is simply for you to spend forever with him.

Maybe today is a good day
to thank God for the gift of eternal life.
No matter what happens to your plans
and the plans of this world,
God's biggest plan will remain.
Forever.

The Light of the World

"I am the
light of the world.
Whoever follows me
will never walk in darkness,
but will have the light of life."

JOHN 8:12

Jesus promised
that we never have to walk in darkness
as long as we follow him.
Talk to him about what it means
to truly follow in his path.
When you do,
you are sure to have light-filled life
wherever you may go.

Overflowing Hope

**May the God of hope
fill you with all joy and peace
as you trust in him,
so that you may overflow with hope
by the power of the Holy Spirit.**

ROMANS 15:13

Ever get discouraged? Wonder what God's up to? Got no clue why you're on this planet? Read Romans 15:13. Now read it again. *Slowly.*

Write out the verse in big letters, hang it where you can see it, and let it bring you hope as you're discovering God's big plans for you.

Hey, YOU!
I've Got Big Plans for

MY BOOK SAYS

"For I know the plans I have for you," declares the Lord, "plans to prosper you and not to harm you, plans to give you hope and a future."

JEREMIAH 29:11

LISTEN REAL CLOSE

When it seems like everyone is taller than you . . .

When it seems that everyone is always telling you what to do . . .

It can be hard to imagine the big plans God has for your life.

But in Jeremiah 29:11, God is talking to YOU.

God has big plans for you, and that verse gives us a few hints about them: "plans to prosper you . . . give you hope and a future."

So the next time you feel like an itty-bitty speck in a humongous world, remember this: God has planted those plans deep in your heart. Right now, they may be tiny seeds that only God can see. But water them with prayer, feed them with God's Word, and warm them by doing God's will. Soon those plans that he planted will grow big enough for everyone to see!

GET TO IT!

Take some time to memorize Jeremiah 29:11.
Whenever you feel like you're not important,
talk to God about his plans for you.
Then, go face this big ol' world knowing
you've got God's plans growing deep in your heart.

I've Given YOU a Purpose

I've given **YOU** a purpose.

You are my hands and my feet
there on earth.
I've given you a purpose—
it's been there since birth!

God has given YOU a purpose that only YOU can do.
Do you know what it is? No?
He's probably given you clues along the way.

Let's take a look.

I've Given Esther a Purpose!

**"Who knows but that you have come
to your royal position for such a time as this?"**

ESTHER 4:14

Mordecai had taken in his cousin Esther because, as the Bible tells us, "she had neither father nor mother" (Esther 2:7). Although Esther was beautiful, she was young, soft-spoken, and, for whatever reason, an orphan. She hardly stood out as a girl with great purpose. Who would ever notice her?

Well, King Xerxes, for one. In fact, a beautiful, soft-spoken young lady was exactly what he was looking for, and he crowned Esther as the next queen.

But even though she was the queen, it was against the law for Esther to approach her king without him calling for her. So when Mordecai sent Esther the news about a plot to kill their family—to kill *all* of the Jews—Esther didn't know what to do. Only the king could stop the evil plan. But if Esther approached the king about it, he could choose to put her to death.

In a final pep talk to Esther, Mordecai told her, "If you don't help your people, God will find some other way to save the Jews. But me, you, our family—we'll all die. Who knows? Maybe this is the very reason you were chosen to be queen."

See, Mordecai knew that God would be faithful to his promise to the Jews, no matter what. But Esther—and her family—could miss out on the purpose God had created just for her. Do you know what Esther did? She mustered her courage, risked her life, and asked the king for his help.

And we're still talking about her today.

Read all about Esther's purpose
in the book of Esther.
Then, take some time to consider where
God has placed you and why.
Perhaps you have been chosen
for such a time as this.

Wonderfully Made

I praise you because I am fearfully and wonderfully made; your works are wonderful, I know that full well.

PSALM 139:14

From the tip of your nose to the bottom of your toes and everything in between,

God crafted you, shaped you, created you, perfectly precisely pristine!

Praise God! YOU are wonderfully made.

Holy and Pleasing?

**Therefore, I urge you, brothers and sisters,
in view of God's mercy,
to offer your bodies as a living sacrifice,
holy and pleasing to God—
this is your true and proper worship.**

ROMANS 12;1

Romans 12:1 gives us a great big hint about our purpose. Fulfilling that purpose will look different for each of us. And it happens one little decision at a time. Ask yourself often, "Is what I'm doing holy and pleasing to God"? If yes, then you're taking another step toward your God-given purpose. If not, well then . . . maybe you should do something else.

RIGHT NOW TALK TO GOD ABOUT WHAT IS HOLY AND PLEASING TO HIM.

God's Instruction Manual

**All Scripture is God-breathed
and is useful for teaching, rebuking,
correcting and training in righteousness,
so that the servant of God may be thoroughly
equipped for every good work.**

2 TIMOTHY 3:16–17

When baking a cake or assembling a model car, you've got to read the instructions, right? What would happen if you didn't? What if you poured a whole gallon of milk into the cake batter? Or what if you decided to use water instead of model glue? You'd have a great big mess.

Well, it's the same with life. To build a life that turns out well, it helps to know what makes things go easier and what messes everything up. God has given you a big book—the Bible—that tells you those things so you will be "equipped for every good work." In it, he's given you examples of what to do and what not to do, and he tells you how people and things work best together.

Reading the directions is not always exciting. It may not be as fun as eating the cake or racing the car. But in the end, following the instructions will give you a life that you can be proud of.

Think about some of God's instructions that you've already learned. Are you following them? Thank God today for providing you with an instruction manual for life.

A Test

Blessed is the one who heeds wisdom's instruction.

PROVERBS 29:18

TEST

1. Read these instructions carefully before you do anything.

2. Read Proverbs 29:18.

3. Write Proverbs 29:18 in purple ink.

4. Turn to page 132 in this book.

5. Turn down the top right corner of page 14.

6. Open and close your book three times.

7. Say, "Blah, blah, blee, blee, bloo, bloo."

8. Now that you've finished reading the instructions, go back and only do number two.

Sooo, how'd you do? If you said "bloo, bloo" at any point in the last few minutes, you probably need to read Proverbs 29:18 again. But if you only completed numbers one and two, great job! You're already pretty good at "heeding" instruction.

The Talking Heart

**I will praise the LORD who counsels me,
even at night my heart instructs me.**

PSALM 16:7

A talking dog, a talking horse,

Maybe a talking work of art,

But who in the world has seen or heard

The likes of a talking heart?

Yet when my heart meets with God's,

When my mind is still and meek,

I suddenly need to do what is right,

And then I know: my heart can speak.

What is your heart saying to you?

Listen ...

Scavenger Hunt!

For everything that was written in the past was written to teach us, so that through the endurance taught in the Scriptures and the encouragement they provide we might have hope.

ROMANS 15:4

The Bible isn't just a long list of rules meant to boss you around. As you read it, you'll also find words to guide you, to encourage you, to give you hope.

Let's have a scavenger hunt right now and do just that. Grab your Bible. See if you can find:

1. One verse of guidance

2. One verse of encouragement

3. One verse that gives you hope

4. Memorize one of those verses today so you can keep it with you always!

Thank God today for his message of hope.

Every Good Path

For the LORD
gives wisdom;
from his mouth come
knowledge and understanding.
He holds success in store for the upright,
he is a shield to those whose walk is blameless,
for he guards the course of the just and protects
the way of his faithful ones. Then you will
understand what is right and just and fair—
every good path.

PROVERBS 2:6–9

Yes, seeking God's guidance will lead you
to your purpose. But walking God's path brings
so much more than that.
Spend some time with Proverbs 2:6–9.
What does God promise to those who walk with him?

"Follow Me"

MATTHEW 4:18–20

Two brothers, Peter and Andrew, were casting a net into the Sea of Galilee when a voice called out to them. "Come on, follow me." As their net hit the water, they looked up to see the man. "I'll send you fishing for people," he added. And with that, Peter and Andrew immediately left their nets and followed Jesus.

When Jesus called his disciples, he went to them. He met them where they were. And his request was always simple, "Follow me."

It's the same today. Jesus is calling you to use your gifts—as a fisher or a teacher or a singer or a friend—to tell others about him, to invite them into his kingdom.

Finding God's purpose for you isn't meant to be difficult. In fact, it's often as simple as obeying those two words:

"FOLLOW ME."

God's Purpose

**He has saved us and
called us to a holy life—
not because of anything we have done
but because of his own purpose and grace.**

2 TIMOTHY 1:9

Even if we don't follow all of the directions . . .

Even if we can't seem to get anything right . . .

Even if we have no clue what our purpose is . . .

It's okay. God has called you to his purpose.

No matter what.

And in the end, it's only God's purpose that truly matters.

Spend some time today discovering
God and his purpose.

A Warrior on Your Side

The Lord your God
is with you,
the Mighty Warrior who saves.

ZEPHANIAH 3:17

Life may get a little bumpy;

You may get lost along the way,

But by your side is a Mighty Warrior,

A Warrior who saves.

Trust in the One
who is always by your side.

It Will Be

The Lord Almighty has sworn,
"Surely, as I have planned,
so it will be,
and as I have purposed,
so it will happen."

ISAIAH 14:24

Relax,

Sigh,

Take a deep breath.

It isn't all up to you.

Pray,

Listen,

Study God's Word.

All of his plans will come true.

Different but the Same

**There are different kinds of gifts,
but the same Spirit distributes them.
There are different kinds of service,
but the same Lord.
There are different kinds of working,
but . . . it is the same God at work.**

1 CORINTHIANS 12:4–6

Your purpose is *YOUR* purpose. It probably won't look like your brother's. It probably will be different from your best friend's. It probably won't be the same as your mom's. But be confident—never doubt for a second—that your God-given purpose is just as important as theirs.

Big or small,
your purpose comes
from the same Spirit,
serves the same Lord,
and is the same
God working within YOU.

I've Given YOU a Purpose!

MY BOOK SAYS

Do not conform to the pattern of this world, but be transformed by the renewing of your mind. Then you will be able to test and approve what God's will is— his good, pleasing and perfect will.

ROMANS 12:2

LISTEN REAL CLOSE

If I can tell you anything about finding your purpose, it's this: Discovering your purpose isn't a one-time thing. It's more like an ongoing, day-by-day, lifelong thing. And just when you think you've fulfilled your purpose, God will give you a new one!

So how can you be sure to stay on track? Well, Romans 12:2 is pretty clear about that. Forget what the world is doing. Don't do things just because they're "in" or popular. By "renewing" your mind (regularly filling your mind with God stuff instead of "world" stuff), you will be prepared to walk daily in your God-given purpose—whatever that may be!

GET TO IT!

Think about the "pattern of this world."
What does the world say about you,
about your looks, your beliefs, your purpose?
Take some time right now to transform yourself,
to renew your mind, by digging into the Bible
and seeing what God says about those things.
Read them, write them down, memorize them.
Replace the patterns of this world
with the truth of your Creator.

I Don't Do Things Small

OHH, it's no little purpose!
(I don't do things small.)
Yours is the most

purpose of all!

No matter how young or how old, how big or how small, YOU have a HUGE purpose! God gave it to you, along with everything you'll need to fulfill that purpose. You're limited only by your beliefs—your belief in God and your belief in yourself. So dream big! Reach for the stars! And believe wholeheartedly in the amazing, astounding, astonishing power of God!

A Little Lunch

JOHN 6:1–13

High on a mountainside overlooking the Sea of Galilee, Jesus sat with his disciples and watched a large crowd approach. With a knowing smile, Jesus elbowed Philip. "Where are we going to buy food for all of these people?"

Philip shook his head. "I could work for six months and still barely have enough for each person to have a bite!"

Then Andrew spoke up, "Over here! This boy has five small loaves and two small fish. But still, how can we feed so many with so little?"

That was exactly the question Jesus was waiting for. "Have the people sit down," he said. And when all five thousand were seated, Jesus took the bread and gave thanks. He did the same with the fish. And the disciples handed out bread and fish to every single person there.

I Don't Do Things Small   63

Jesus looked across the mountainside and saw the faces of five thousand people filled with God's abundance. He told his disciples, "Be sure to gather what's left over. We don't want anything wasted."

As the disciples gathered the food, they grew more and more amazed. After feeding five thousand people, the leftovers from those five little loaves and two little fish filled twelve baskets with food.

What do you have to offer God today?
No matter how small it seems,
pick up your basket and hand it over to God.
Together, you'll do the most humongous things of all.

WHAT DO YOU HAVE
TO OFFER GOD TODAY?

Just a Kid

**Don't let anyone look down on you
because you are young, but set an example
for the believers in speech, in conduct,
in love, in faith and in purity.**

1 TIMOTHY 4:12

"Maybe one day, sweetie."

"You're not tall enough."

"You're just a kid."

Okay, so maybe you're not old enough to have a driver's license or tall enough to ride the roller coaster. But don't ever, ever believe that you're just a kid.

Kids are a big deal to God! Psalm 127:3 even says that children are a "reward" from him.

That's right: YOU are a gift to this world!

And 1 Timothy 4:12 says that even when you're young, you are to set an example for others: in the way you talk, in the way you act, in the way you treat others, and in your walk with God.

YOU matter.

The way you talk and act and treat others matters. The way you worship matters. No matter how young or small or quiet, YOU are leading the way for others with your example.

Make it count.

Kid David

1 SAMUEL 17

David was "just a kid" when his father sent him to carry food to his brothers on the battlefield. When David got to the camp, he heard a voice booming up from the valley, and then he watched as the Israelite army scattered like insects.

"Who is that guy?" David asked. "And who does he think he is talking to the Lord's army that way?!"

It wasn't just any guy. It was Goliath, an almost-ten-foot-tall warrior. But unlike the Israelite army, David wasn't impressed by Goliath's height or his age or his threats.

Without armor or sword or shield, David went out to face Goliath. Armed with only a shepherd's staff, a sling, and five smooth stones, young David faced the giant who had frightened an entire army

Of course, David defeated the giant that day—not because David was bigger, stronger, older, or wiser than Goliath, but because David was fighting for the Lord.

Face your giants today by
fighting in the name of the Lord.

Greater Than

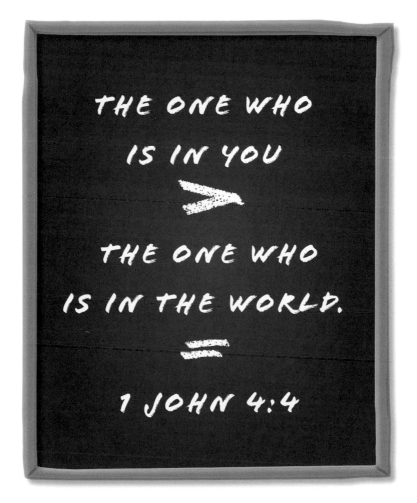

THE ONE WHO

IS IN YOU

>

THE ONE WHO

IS IN THE WORLD.

=

1 JOHN 4:4

You do the math.

What is God telling you in 1 John 4:4?

This is one math problem that you can use—

every day of your life.

What Do You Need?

**And God is able to bless you abundantly,
so that in all things at all times,
having all that you need,
you will abound in every good work.**

2 CORINTHIANS 9:8

"I'd do it, if only I had . . ."

How would you complete that sentence? You know, God is able to provide everything you need to do his work.

Talk to God about what he wants you to do.

Ask him for the tools you'll need to get it done.

Then gear up, get out there, and get busy!

Mustard-Seed Faith

**"Truly I tell you, if you have faith as small
as a mustard seed, you can say to this mountain,
'Move from here to there,' and it will move.
Nothing will be impossible for you."**

MATTHEW 17:20

Have you ever seen a mustard seed? It's teeny tiny—about the size of a sesame seed on a hamburger bun. And yet, this is how big Jesus said your faith needs to be in order to move mountains.

What do you want to do today? What seems impossible to you? Is it bigger than moving a mountain? No? Then I believe you have just enough faith to get the job done.

Go! Put that mustard-seed faith to work
and move mountains today!

His Riches Are Yours

And my God will meet all your
needs according to the riches
of his glory in Christ Jesus.

PHILIPPIANS 4:19

Thank God for his riches today.
How can you use them toward
the plans he has for YOU?

Count the grains of sand on the shore,
each sparkling star in the night.
Count the number of fish in the sea,
snowflakes in a blanket of white.

Count the blades of grass on a hill,
the leaves high up in the tree.
All the riches of heaven and earth,
God offers to you and me.

Nothing Is
Too Big for God

EXODUS 14

Moses looked back at thousands of people waiting for his answer. On one side of the Israelites, the enormous Red Sea rolled out far and wide. On the other side, Egyptian soldiers were churning up clouds of dust as they charged toward God's people with full force.

Will we die by the sea or the sword? the Israelites must have been wondering. Some even dared to blame Moses for their sure-to-be-terrible fate.

"Just watch," Moses told them, "the Lord will save us."

And God did.

But God didn't do things small. Oh nooo . . . God took that enormous Red Sea and split it right down the middle. He even dried up the soggy seafloor! And the Israelites crossed over to safety, on dry land, in the middle of the Red Sea.

God didn't do things small then. And he doesn't now.
Instead of cowering in fear,
instead of blaming others for your fate,
have a little faith and expect
HUMONGOUS
things to happen in your life.

Big Thoughts

**"For my thoughts are not your thoughts,
neither are your ways my ways,"
declares the LORD.**

ISAIAH 55:8

What is God thinking?

Why does he
do what he does?

We may never know
except for this:

God wants the best—and he wants it

BIG!

Super-Powered Prayers

"If you believe, you will receive whatever you ask for in prayer."

MATTHEW 21:22

Most of us don't realize just how powerful our prayers are. But check out the verse above. Jesus said it himself!

Now, I don't think he was talking about asking for gifts and gadgets. But I do know that if Jesus said it, he meant it. And it's undeniably true.

So put this into practice. Pray for your brother. Pray for your teacher. Pray for your hamster. Pray for your lemonade stand. Pray for your skinned knee.

Just pray. Believe. And watch in wonder as your super-powered prayers change lives.

If You Can?

MARK 9:14–29

A man came up to Jesus in the street. "Teacher, my son is possessed by a terrible spirit. He can't speak. The spirit throws him to the ground, and he foams at the mouth, gnashes his teeth, and becomes stiff as a board."

As the disciples listened next to Jesus, they braced themselves. They knew what was coming next. "I asked your disciples to help us," the father continued, "but they couldn't do it."

EVERYTHING IS POSSIBLE
WHEN YOU
BELIEVE

Jesus turned to them. "You unbelievers . . ." he shook his head. "Bring the boy to me."

When they brought the boy to Jesus, he immediately fell to the ground just as his father had described.

"How long has he been like this?" Jesus asked.

"Since he was a child. Sometimes it even throws him into water or fire," the father explained. "Please, if you can do anything, help us."

Now let's pause this story for a second. How do you respond when someone says, "If you can . . . "? Do you take it as a challenge? Or do you mumble, "I'll tryyyy . . . "?

I love how Jesus responds.

"'If you can?" said Jesus. "Everything is possible when you believe."

His reply says so much. First, Jesus seems to be unfamiliar with the term "if." It's almost as though the phrase "if you can" seems silly to him. And second, of course, Jesus states the one fact that is a game-changer for all of our plans: Belief makes everything possible.

So the next time you start to stick
an "if" in God's plans, remember Jesus' response.
Within God's plans for you,
there's no room for such a silly little word.

How Big Is God's Love?

And I pray that you,
being rooted and established
in love, may have power, together
with all the Lord's holy people,
to grasp how wide and long
and high and deep is
the love of Christ.

EPHESIANS 3:17–18

God doesn't do things small.
And perhaps the thing he does biggest of all is

LOVE.

Wrap your mind and heart around the verse above.

Just try to imagine God's love.

You Were Planned Long Ago

**LORD, you are my God;
I will exalt you and praise your name,
for in perfect faithfulness
you have done wonderful things,
things planned long ago.**

ISAIAH 25:1

Long, long ago, when the earth was brand-new,
God came up with the idea of YOU.

"Oh, this is a good one!" he said with a smile.
"Yep, this one just may take me a while."

Ever since then, with his very own hands,
God has been crafting your wonderful plans.

They may take time
and hard work to come true,
But God has HUMONGOUS plans
just for YOU.

Little Things

MY BOOK SAYS

*"His master replied,
'Well done, good and faithful servant!
You have been faithful with a few things;
I will put you in charge of many things.'"*

MATTHEW 25:21

LISTEN REAL CLOSE

Maybe you're doing some humongous things right now. Or maybe your efforts still look pretty small. But through the parable in Matthew 25, Jesus reminds us to be faithful, to work hard on the little things too. Those little things may seem like they don't matter at the moment, but God will use them to prepare us for the bigger things that lie ahead.

GET TO IT!

Think about some things you're currently working on.
(Write them down, if you'd like.)
Maybe you're improving an art skill
or trying to stop biting your nails
or remembering to feed your pet every day.
Try to think of at least three things.
Now, think about (or write next to each one)
how God could be using each of those things
to prepare you for something HUGE.
Use Matthew 25:21 to motivate you
to do your best in the little things.

There's Nothing YOU Can't Do

There's nothing YOU can't do!

**I can do all things
through Christ who strengthens me.**

PHILIPPIANS 4:13 (NKJV)

What's one thing that has caused
you to whisper,
"I can't"?
What does God say about that?
Maybe you could try again?

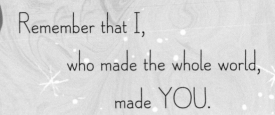

Remember that I,
who made the whole world,
made YOU.

And there's nothing that,
with my help,
YOU can't do!

There's Nothing YOU Can't Do! 85

"I Will Be with You."

S o we've all heard the story of Moses standing tall by the Red

EXODUS 3–4

Sea, stretching his staff across the brewing waters just before they went shooting into the sky. Then Moses miraculously led hundreds of thousands of Israelites straight through the middle of the sea—on dry land—until they were safe on the other side. It's a pretty heroic story, right?

But have you heard the one about Moses the chicken? No?

Well, let's skip back in time a bit. Let's go back before Moses and the Red Sea, before the ten plagues on the Egyptians, and all the way back to when Moses tended the flocks for his father-in-law, Jethro. Moses had just led the flock to the edge of the wilderness, when he saw a bush burning on the mountain. As he watched, he noticed something odd: the bush wasn't burning up. So he went to get a closer look.

As Moses got closer, the bush called out to him, "Moses! Moses!"

And what did Moses do? He answered the bush, "I'm here."

Then Moses learned he wasn't talking to a bush at all; he was talking to God.

"Moses, my people are miserable in Egypt. I'm sending you to lead them out of there."

And that's when Moses turned chicken.

"Waaait a minute, God. Why do you want to send me? Who am I to lead the Israelites?" The last time Moses was in Egypt, he'd been running for his life. And now God wanted to send him back there?

God's answer was simple: "I will be with you" (Exodus 3:12).

Moses didn't grasp the hugeness of God's statement. "But—but who do I tell them you are? And what if they don't believe me? What if they don't even listen to me?"

So God gave Moses the power to perform miraculous signs so the Israelites would believe that God had sent Moses to them.

"But, God, even with that, you see, I've never been much of a public speaker. I speak slowly, I mumble, I, I—"

"Who created the human mouth? Who makes people hear? Who gives them sight? It is me, and I will be with you."

"Pardon me, God, but well, I . . . you see . . . would you please just send someone else?"

"Okay, Moses. Your brother Aaron will help you. He's already on his way here. I will be with both of you. I'll tell you what to say. I'll teach you what to do. I. Will. Be. With. You."

And you know what? God was. He was with Moses and Aaron the first, second, and all the way through the tenth time they approached Pharaoh. God was with Moses and Aaron and all of the Israelites when the frogs, flies, and locusts swept across the land of Egypt. And God was right there with Moses as he stood tall, stretched out his hand, and parted the Red Sea for God's people to cross over to safety.

What excuses do you make to God?
No excuse can stand in the way
of the plans God has for you.
Just remember Exodus 3:12.
He will be with you.

"Look to the Lord"

1 CHRONICLES 16:11

Look to the Lord and his strength; seek his face always.

What are you looking for? Love? Strength? Friends? Happiness? Take a cue from 1 Chronicles 16:11 and look to the Lord, allow his strength to fuel you, and seek him always. In him, you will find everything you're looking for ... and so much more.

Mustard-Seed Faith

**"If you have faith as small as a mustard seed,
you can say to this mulberry tree,
'Be uprooted and planted in the sea,'
and it will obey you."**

LUKE 17:6

Why do you think Jesus said this to his disciples? Do you think he wanted them to change the landscape? To rearrange the mulberry trees?

Hmm ... probably not.

I'd say Jesus wanted them to feed their faith.

I'd say he wanted them to empty their hearts of doubt.

I'd say he wanted them to fill their hearts with belief ... and to imagine what was possible when they did.

And I'd say Jesus is saying the very same thing to you and me.

What can you do to fill your heart with faith—
today and every day?

The Secret to Success

**Plans fail for lack of counsel,
but with many advisers they succeed.**

PROVERBS 15:22

What are your big plans?

Have you talked to God about those plans?

Who else do you look to for help?

Don't let your plans fail because of a lack of good advice. Seek God's guidance first, and be sure to listen to him speaking through the older, wiser people he has placed around you.

Choose the right advisers.
With many advisers, your plans will succeed!

He Will Provide

As you grow and learn,

    as you try to follow the plans God has for you,

        remember that he is always there

            supplying everything you need

                to grow strong and wise in his ways.

What do you need?

Just tell him.

He will provide.

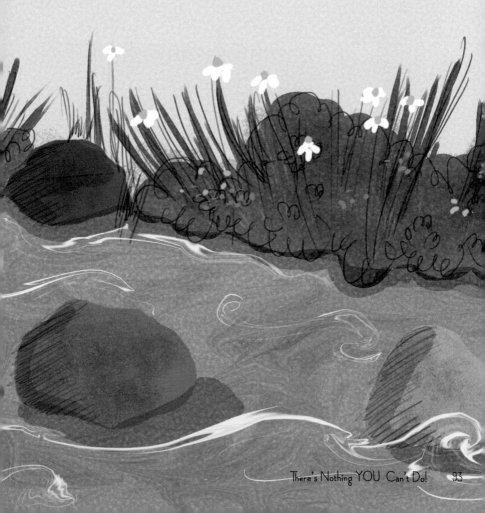

"The Lord will guide you continually,
and satisfy your needs in parched places,
and make your bones strong;
and you shall be like a watered garden,
like a spring of water,
whose waters never fail."

ISAIAH 58:11 (NRS)

To the One Who Knocks

**When the disciples asked Jesus how to pray,
he explained, "Ask and it will be given to you;
seek and you will find;
knock and the door will be opened to you.
For everyone who asks receives;
the one who seeks finds;
and to the one who knocks,
the door will be opened"**

LUKE 11:9–10

I t doesn't get any simpler than that, does it? God wants you to ask, to seek, and to knock. When you do, the door will open, you will receive, and you will find.

Take your requests
to the door of Jesus and knock.

"Come to Me"

Jesus said, "Let the little children come to me, and do not hinder them, for the kingdom of heaven belongs to such as these."

MATTHEW 19:14

If you've ever thought that big plans were just for adults, that you weren't big enough to do God's work, that Jesus calls only the grownups, then spend some time with the verse above.

Jesus invites you to come to him. He reminds the grownups not to get in the way. And he offers the kingdom of heaven to children just like you.

Jesus is calling you.
Will you come to him?

Bear Fruit

"I am the vine; you are the branches.
If you remain in me and I in you,
you will bear much fruit;
apart from me you can do nothing."

JOHN 15:5

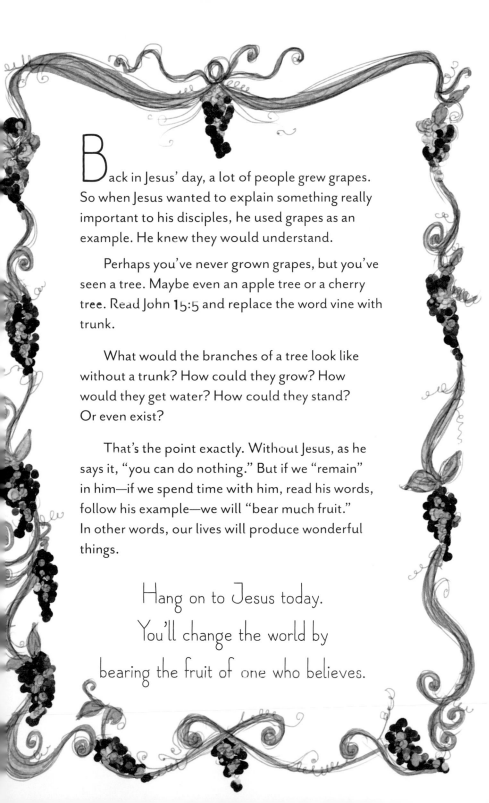

Back in Jesus' day, a lot of people grew grapes. So when Jesus wanted to explain something really important to his disciples, he used grapes as an example. He knew they would understand.

Perhaps you've never grown grapes, but you've seen a tree. Maybe even an apple tree or a cherry tree. Read John 15:5 and replace the word vine with trunk.

What would the branches of a tree look like without a trunk? How could they grow? How would they get water? How could they stand? Or even exist?

That's the point exactly. Without Jesus, as he says it, "you can do nothing." But if we "remain" in him—if we spend time with him, read his words, follow his example—we will "bear much fruit." In other words, our lives will produce wonderful things.

Hang on to Jesus today.
You'll change the world by
bearing the fruit of one who believes.

Spirit Muscles

**I pray that out of his glorious riches
he may strengthen you with power
through his Spirit in your inner being.**

EPHESIANS 3:16

When you think about being big and strong, you're usually thinking about your outside: your height, your weight, your muscles. But in Ephesians, Paul prays that your insides will be strong. He wants you to rely on God's endless power to strengthen your Spirit.

What does that mean, exactly? Well, it means that you rely on God to tell you what's right and wrong. You act when something inside of you whispers, "Help her." You tell God you're sorry when you've done something wrong. All of those things are exercises that will keep your Spirit muscles big and strong.

Be sure to give your inner being a workout
—today and every day.

God Gave YOU Power!

**For the Spirit God gave us does not make us timid,
but gives us power, love and self-discipline.**

2 TIMOTHY 1:7

Reach down,
    Way down deep.
        You feel that?
            That strength?

The power of God
    Is there—inside,
        Not meant to be wasted,
            Not meant to hide.

Let it shine out,
    bright and loud!
        Use your power,
            strong and proud!

Faith Over Fear

MATTHEW 14:22–33

Remember the story of Moses the chicken? (See "I Will Be with You" on page 86.) Well, hundreds of years later, Jesus' disciple, Peter, pulled a chicken move too. However, just before that, he did something that required huge faith. And through it all, Jesus shows us that whether our faith is huge or chicken-like, he'll be there to pull us through (or up, as in Peter's case).

There's Nothing YOU Can't Do!   101

Go back with me to the Sea of Galilee. It was the middle of the night, and it had been a long, crazy day. The disciples had passed around a bottomless basket of fish and bread to feed more than five thousand people. (See A Little Lunch on page 62.) And now, headed to their next assignment, the disciples were in a boat that was being battered by the wind and waves. To add to the excitement, they noticed a strange figure walking across the water . . . and it was headed straight for them.

"AAaaggh! A ghost!" they cried.

The "ghost" answered. "Hey, guys, don't be afraid. It's just me."

Peter recognized the voice and mustered his courage. "Lord, if it is you, tell me to come out there."

"Come."

At that simple invitation, Peter stepped out of the boat. Against the wind, the waves, the darkness, and his fear, Peter stood on top of the roaring water and walked toward his Savior.

Imagine that for a minute. Feel the wind blowing; hear the waves crashing. You're barely able to see the figure, much less hear his one-word reply. Is it really Jesus? The other eleven disciples were probably yelling, "Peter! Don't do it, man! You don't know what's out there! Are you sure that's Jesus? Are you sure he called you? It's much safer here in the boat!"

And still Peter walked. On the water. To Jesus.

When Peter got out there, however, he realized what he'd done.

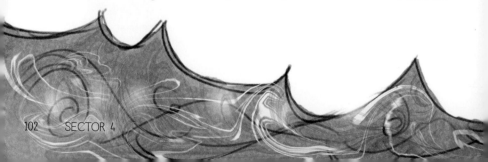

He felt the wind, saw the water, and fear overtook his faith. Peter began to sink.

"Jesus! Save me!"

Jesus caught him; the Bible says "immediately." But instead of questioning the wind or the waves for letting Peter sink, Jesus turned to Peter: "You of little faith . . . why did you doubt?" (verse 31).

Together, Peter and Jesus stepped into the boat, and the wind died down. After seeing all of this, those in the boat worshiped Jesus, saying, "Truly you are the Son of God" (verse 33).

The disciples had been afraid of the waves and the wind and the darkness. But Jesus knew none of that stuff mattered. Jesus knew that doubt was the one thing that had caused Peter to sink—and faith was the only thing that could overcome it all.

Thanks to Peter's willingness to step out in faith—and even thanks to his chicken move—we learn something important about our power in Jesus. While Peter was focused on Jesus, he was able to do the miraculous. But when he looked toward the powers working against him, Peter sank into waves of fear. And even though Peter's fear caused him to sink, Jesus was willing to lift him up again.

Whether you're sinking or stepping out, choose faith over fear today. When you do, you'll discover the miraculous abilities you have in Jesus.

The Peace of God

**And the peace of God,
which transcends all understanding,
will guard your hearts and your minds
in Christ Jesus.**

PHILIPPIANS 4:7

When you walk with God, you are not only promised great power. You are not only promised that God will supply your needs. But along with all of that, you are also promised a peace that surpasses understanding.

It's a peace that will fill your heart when you're sad or angry. It's a peace that protects your mind when you're worried or anxious. It's a peace that you won't even understand. But it's there. It's yours. And it will guard you when you entrust your life to God.

Feel the peace of God protecting your heart today.

God's Reflection

So God created mankind in his own image,
in the image of God he created them.

GENESIS 1:27

Have you ever seen God?
How big is he?
Does he look like a cloud?
Or a hickory tree?

God said it twice, so I
Know that it's true:
We're made in his image—
Yes, me and you!

As you meet others in life,
Never forget:
YOU reflect the God that
They may not have met.

Nothing YOU Can't Do!

MY BOOK SAYS

**With God's power working in us,
God can do much, much more
than anything we can ask or imagine.**

EPHESIANS 3:20 (NCV)

LISTEN REAL CLOSE

Your wildest dreams.

Your craziest goals.

Your prayer of all prayers.

Poof! It's all yours.

But wait, there's more! Much, much more. "More than anything we can ask or imagine."

That's the power of God. That's the power of God working in you. When you set your sails toward God's horizon, he'll get you there. When you listen to God when he calls, you'll always be happy you said yes. When you trust God with your plans, he'll make them all come true and so much more.

GET TO IT!

Make a list of the big plans you have for your life.

Be sure to focus on the plans
God has for your life too.

Include at least one thing that's so awesomely huge that
you could never ever accomplish it on your own.

Now read your list knowing that—with God—
you can do all of those things
and "much, much more."

Find That ONE Thing

FIND THAT ONE THING

So open your heart
and listen real close.
You'll find that one thing
that you love the most.

What do you love to do?

What do you do really well?

What has God
created you to do?

Keep looking.
Together, we'll start to uncover
the one thing that
inspires you the most.

Noah's One Thing

GENESIS 6–8

The Bible says Noah was a "righteous" and "blameless" man; "he walked faithfully with God" (Genesis 6:9). So when God was fed up and ready to destroy all of the wickedness in the world, he turned to Noah.

"I am going to bring floodwaters on the earth to destroy all life under the heavens . . . Everything on earth will perish. But I will establish my covenant with you, and you will enter the ark—you and your sons and your wife and your sons' wives with you" (Genesis 6:17–18). God then explained how Noah would also save two of every kind of animal by bringing them onto the ark.

The "one thing" God had tasked Noah with was the survival of life on planet earth. It was kind of an important task! But with Noah's obedience and God's power and guidance, another miracle would be recorded on the pages of our Bible.

You probably know the rest of the story. As God directed, Noah built a huge boat—more than ten school buses long—and loaded his family and the animals on board for a long boat ride. It rained for forty days straight, and the waters "lifted the ark high above the earth" (Genesis 7:17). Even the mountains were completely covered, and everything on earth died—everything but those people and animals Noah had brought into the ark with him.

Several months later, when God said it was time, Noah, his family, and all the animals stepped off the ark onto dry land. Together, they would be the new beginning of the world.

What will your one thing be?
How will your one thing change the world?
Trust God to show you the way.

Different Gifts

**We have different gifts,
according to the grace given to each of us.**

ROMANS 12:6

From the greatest speaker to the best listener, from the wisest teacher to the most eager student, we each are given very different gifts. Yet they all come from the very same God.

Don't worry if your gift doesn't look like everyone else's. Every gift is important; each person must play his or her part. And big things happen when all of God's gifts work together for his glory.

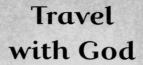

Travel with God

**Your word is a
lamp for my feet,
a light on my path.**

PSALM 119:105

Do you ever wonder which way to go?
Ever think you've lost your way?
God's Word will bring wisdom and light
Even to the darkest of days!

Always travel with God
and rely on God's Word to light your way!

Step Strong!

**The Lord makes firm the steps
of the one who delights in him.**

PSALM 37:23

When you're worn and weary,
And it feels like you can't go on,
Turn to the Lord, find joy in him,
And your steps will be sure and strong!

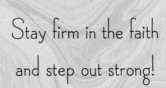

Stay firm in the faith
and step out strong!

Teamwork
Builds a Tabernacle

EXODUS 35–36

When God gave Moses the Ten Commandments, he gave him another set of instructions too. Moses was to lead the Israelites in building a tabernacle—a church—where the people could worship and come together with God.

Moses told them, "From what you have, take an offering for the LORD" (Exodus 35:5). And the people brought everything from spices and oil to gold and fine jewels. Even after work had begun on the Holy Tent, the people kept bringing gifts every morning until finally the workers said to Moses, "Tell the people to stop bringing gifts—we have more than enough!"

For the construction of the tabernacle, Moses told them, "All who are skilled among you are to come and make everything the

LORD has commanded" (Exodus 35:10). So the people came, each with his or her own skill, and together they built God's holy tabernacle.

When God called for materials, some brought olive oil; others brought precious jewels. And together they had more than enough. When he called for workers, some spun goat hair into thread; others crafted items of gold. And together they created a place where they could worship God as one.

God doesn't ask for more than what we have.
He doesn't require us to have any more skill
than what he's given to us.
Be like that generous giver and that skilled worker;
give so much that someone has to
stop you from bringing more.
And together we'll work to build the kingdom of God.

A Word to the Not-So-Wise

**If any of you lacks wisdom, you should ask God,
who gives generously to all without finding fault,
and it will be given to you.**

JAMES 1:5

See that word up there? The one between to and without? Yeah, that one. All. Do you know what that means?

It means that none of us—not even those who are young—have an excuse for lacking wisdom. God will give it to us generously. He's willing to give it to all of us. We just have to ask.

So if you're feeling a little lost, a little lacking, a little out of the loop—go straight to the top. Just call on the God of knowledge, the God of wisdom, the God who's all-knowing and simply ask.

Ask him, believing that he will
generously give wisdom to all.
And that includes YOU.

Look with Your Heart

**You will seek me and find me
when you seek me with all your heart.**

JEREMIAH 29:13

Where is God?

Where can you find him?

Where do you go when you need to talk to him?

If you're not sure, then God has an answer for you. And it's simple. When you look for God, you'll find him. But no halfhearted hide-and-seek will do. God says to seek him "with all your heart." If you want to know God—and you mean it—he will reveal to you all that you want to know.

Seek him.
With your whole heart.
And there, you will find him.

What **YOU** are seeking?

"But seek first his kingdom and his righteousness, and all these things will be given to you as well."

MATTHEW 6:33

Instead of seeking money or fame,
Or whatever the world calls "success,"
Look for God's will and his way,
And he will take care of the rest!

WHAT ARE YOU SEEKING FIRST?

What do you spend the most time doing?

What do you dedicate your days to?

Jesus says here that if you put him first
and try to do what is right,
God will meet your needs
and the desires of your heart.
Seek him first today.

All the Days

One thing I ask from the Lord,
this only do I seek:
that I may dwell in the house of the Lord
all the days of my life.

PSALM 27:4

Be sure that your plans for this life factor in your plans for the next. (See The Biggest Plan on page 30.) Even though the future seems like a long, long way away, everything you do today will affect your life forever.

Keep that in mind with what you're seeking. Be sure you're seeking not only what is good for your future, but most importantly, what is best for your eternity.

Pray At All Times

**Be joyful
because you have hope.
Be patient
when trouble comes,
and pray
at all times.**

ROMANS 12:12 (NCV)

No matter what may
come your way today,
You can handle it all,
if you will just pray.

Your Shepherd

The LORD is my shepherd, I lack nothing.
He makes me lie down in green pastures,
he leads me beside quiet waters,
he refreshes my soul.
He guides me along the right paths
for his name's sake.
Even though I walk through the darkest valley,
I will fear no evil, for you are with me;
your rod and your staff, they comfort me.
You prepare a table before me
in the presence of my enemies.
You anoint my head with oil; my cup overflows.
Surely your goodness and love will follow me
all the days of my life,
and I will dwell
in the house of the LORD forever.

PSALM 23

As you follow Jesus,

His love will follow you,

All the days of your life.

Sweet Wisdom

**Know also that wisdom is like honey for you:
If you find it, there is a future hope for you,
and your hope will not be cut off.**

PROVERBS 24:14

If seeking God is the bread of life,
then wisdom is the honey.
Make life a little sweeter by seeking true wisdom—
wisdom that comes from the Word of God.

"Call to Me"

"Call to me and I will answer you and tell you great and unsearchable things you do not know."

JEREMIAH 33:3

You may not always find your way,

Know what to do or what to say,

Or who to trust or where to go,

Or even what you're supposed to know!

But one thing that is sure and true:

Call on God, and he will answer you.

He knows it all and wants to share!

Call him. Trust him. He'll be there.

Your One Thing

MY BOOK SAYS

**In the same way,
let your light shine before others,
that they may see your good deeds
and glorify your Father in heaven.**

MATTHEW 5:16

LISTEN REAL CLOSE

It can be tough to figure out why we're on this planet and exactly what we're supposed to be doing while we're here. But we do know some things for sure: We should seek God first, we should seek true wisdom, and God will be with us no matter what.

When you do find "that one thing that you love the most," that thing you know God wants you to be doing—let it shine. When we do good deeds and use our God-given gifts, it brings glory to God. We can tell everyone how wonderful God is without saying a single word.

GET TO IT!

Pick one thing that you know you're good at, that you know God created you to do, and do that one thing today. Whether or not you realize it, people are watching. And you—yes, little ol' YOU—are bringing glory to God.

What I Created YOU To Do

What I Created YOU to Do

The whole world will be better,
thanks to little ol' you . . .
all because you did what
I CREATED YOU to do.

Wanna change the world?

Start with the One who made it! When you partner with God and work for his purpose, little ol' you can make a huge difference in this big ol' world.

Think about it,
and talk to God about how, together,
you can make the world a better place.

What God Created Gideon to Do

JUDGES 6–7

It's now a couple hundred years since Moses triumphantly led God's people, the Israelites, out of Egypt. But we find the Israelites in a very different state. In fact, they don't look much like God's people at all. They're cowering in the mountains and hiding in caves, trying to keep away from their big-bully neighbors, the Midianites.

The Midianites were so numerous that when they passed through the land, they devoured the Israelites' crops "like swarms of locusts" (verse 5). They also took cows, sheep, and donkeys until the Israelites were left with no food—nothing. That's when the Israelites called out to God.

And God answered by sending an angel to Gideon. "The Lord is with you, mighty warrior," he said (verse 12).

But instead of being grateful or relieved, Gideon answered, "If the Lord is with us, then why are we still being pushed around by Midian?"

God answered simply, "Isn't that what I'm doing—sending you to save Israel?"

"Waaait a minute, Lord," Gideon began. "My clan is the weakest in our tribe, and I am the smallest in my family. How can you send me to save Israel?" "I will be with you." (Sound familiar? See "I Will Be with You" on page 86.)

And boy, was he ever!

After Gideon gathered all of his warriors, God said, "You have too many men. I want Israel to know they were saved by me, not by their own strength."

So Gideon reduced his men from 32,000 to only 10,000.

But God said, "That's still too many men. Take them down to the water to drink, and I'll show you which ones to keep." Gideon did. "See the ones drinking water from cupped hands?" God said. "Keep them and send the others home." When Gideon had again done as God instructed, he counted the remaining men. There were only 300 left.

"Now you're ready," God said. Then he gave Gideon instructions on exactly how to defeat those Midianites.

"Okay, guys, just follow my lead," Gideon said, and he marched his 300 men to the edge of the Midianite camp. Armed with only a trumpet, a clay jar, and a torch, each man followed Gideon's lead. They blew their trumpets, smashed their clay jars, and held their torches high. "A sword for the Lord and for Gideon!" they shouted (verse 20). And then they watched in amazement as the terrified, big-bully Midianites screamed and scattered like mice.

God used Gideon to defeat the Midianites that day. To the world—and even to himself—Gideon may have looked like the smallest man in the weakest clan. But God saw a "mighty warrior" because that's what he had created Gideon to be.

God has created you for a purpose.
Say yes when he calls.
You never know
what'll happen next!

God in You

For it is God who works in you to will and to act in order to fulfill his good purpose.

PHILIPPIANS 2:13

God created YOU—in his image.

He is with you, working in you, guiding you,

waiting for you to listen and obey and act

to help his people

and fulfill his purpose.

Allow God to work through YOU today!

What Is Good

"Why spend money on what is not bread,
and your labor on what does not satisfy?
Listen, listen to me, and eat what is good,
and you will delight in the richest of fare."

ISAIAH 55:2

God's way may not always seem like the easiest …

or the most fun …

or the most rewarding.

Yet he promises that if we listen to him,

we will enjoy the "richest of fare"

that life has to offer.

What I Created YOU To Do

The Lord's Purpose

Many are the plans in a person's heart,
but it is the LORD's purpose that prevails.

PROVERBS 19:21

Nurse? Firefighter? Architect? Teacher? What do you want to be when you grow up?

There are so many options out there—endless possibilities to choose from. As you make plans for your life, big or small, the very first step is to get God's approval. Without his approval, you'll never truly succeed or find happiness.

Only with God will your plans succeed.

Rules for Life

"But be very careful
to keep the commandment
and the law that Moses
the servant of the Lord gave you:
to love the Lord your God,
to walk in obedience to him,
to keep his commands,
to hold fast to him
and to serve him with all your heart
and with all your soul."

JOSHUA 22:5

As you learn more about God and the Bible, it's pretty normal to get confused or bogged down in all the details, opinions, and advice you'll hear from other people about what it all means. But God's Word makes it really clear what we're supposed to do in order to serve him. As long as we're following his Word, we can be confident that we are walking in the plans God has for us.

Hang in there. You've got this.
Stick with God, and he'll take you
exactly where you're supposed to be.

Eye on You

**I will instruct you and teach you
in the way you should go;
I will counsel you with my loving eye on you.**

PSALM 32:8

How awesome, how comforting,

how humbling, how utterly astounding

it is to know

that the God of the universe

is your teacher,

that the Creator of creation

is your counselor,

and that an all-powerful, ever-present King

is right there beside you,

guiding and watching and loving you—

yes, YOU!

Never ever forget to whom you belong.
Today you must know, without a doubt,
that you are his.
God is looking out for YOU.

Washing Feet

JOHN 13

Back in Jesus' day, feet could get pretty nasty. People wore sandals on dirt roads and didn't bathe as often as we do today. So when Jesus—the teacher and leader whom the disciples followed and admired—knelt down to wash their feet, they were shocked.

Peter even refused, "No, you will never wash my feet!"

But Jesus insisted. And after washing their feet, he instructed them, "Just as I have washed your feet, you should wash each other's feet."

While I'm sure your friends would enjoy a good foot bath, Jesus was setting an example for his disciples—and us—to serve others. No matter how old or rich or important we may feel, we're expected to kneel down and serve one another.

Follow Jesus' example
and find a way to serve someone today.

Jonah's Plan

JONAH 1–2

Do you remember the story of Jonah? Yeah, the guy who spent a few days in the belly of a big fish. Do you know how he got there?

He made his own plans.

You see, God had sent Jonah to deliver a message to the wicked city of Nineveh. But Jonah didn't like God's plan. So he ran. He hopped on a ship and sailed in the opposite direction.

Needless to say, Jonah's plan didn't work. God sent a storm so strong the ship started to break apart. When Jonah finally admitted to the ship's crew that the storm was all his fault, they did as Jonah instructed and threw him overboard. When Jonah hit the water, the storm stopped, and a huge fish swallowed him whole.

It was only after Jonah called out to God—after sitting in a stinky fish stomach for three days—that the fish spit Jonah onto dry land. When Jonah agreed to cooperate with God's plan, Jonah was on his way again.

When you get stuck,
when things start to stink—
stop and think.
Maybe it's time to ask yourself,
who's plan am I following?

Run!

**Let us run with perseverance
the race marked out for us,
fixing our eyes on Jesus,
the pioneer and perfecter of faith.**

HEBREWS 12:1–2

Things are going to get hard. You are going to want to quit. You are going to feel like there's no way out, no way you could ever win.

And that's when, more than ever before, you have to fix your eyes on Jesus. That's when you memorize Philippians 4:13 and scream it from the top of your lungs: "I can do all this through him who gives me strength!"

RUN THIS RACE WITH
PERSEVERANCE.
JESUS HAS ALREADY GONE BEFORE YOU.
AND HIS STRENGTH
IS IN YOU TOO.

Move!

**Then the LORD said to Moses,
"Why are you crying out to me?
Tell the Israelites to move on."**

EXODUS 14:15

So many times we beg God for change

    Or to please make our plans come true!

But as you pray, do you ever ask,

    "Is this something I can already do?"

When you've prayed till you cannot pray anymore,

    When the options just leave you confused,

When it seems there's nothing else to be done,

    Maybe God is telling you, "MOVE!"

Go!

When Jesus rose from the dead, he spent forty precious days on earth giving final instructions to his followers. Some of the last words he spoke, before returning to heaven, were these:

"Therefore go and make disciples of all nations,
baptizing them in the name of the Father
and of the Son and of the Holy Spirit,
and teaching them to obey everything
I have commanded you.
And surely I am with you always,
to the very end of the age."

MATTHEW 28:19–20

Right then and there, over two thousand years ago, Jesus revealed the plans that God has for you. If you do nothing else in this world, let this be your plan. Share this amazing message with the whole world —that God is in us and with us and for us.

And know that no matter what you do, God's Spirit is right there with you, "to the very end of the age."

Now ... go ...
tell the world about
the plans God has for them!

For Ever and Ever

**For this God is our God for ever and ever;
he will be our guide even to the end.**

PSALM 48:14

Hundreds of years before Jesus spoke those words to his disciples (see Go! on page 150), this psalmist wrote a strikingly similar message.

Don't you see? This God—the one who created YOU, who is watching over you—has always been here. He knows everything. He is working for YOUR good. And he has a plan for your life.

He has big plans for YOU.

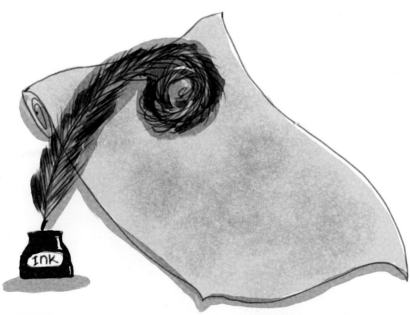

What Is Eternal

So we fix our eyes
not on what is seen,
but on what is unseen,
since what is seen is temporary,
but what is unseen is eternal.

2 CORINTHIANS 4:18

Take a look around. What do you see?

Trees, houses, mailboxes, flowers. TVs, sandwiches, bicycles, games, light poles, cars, rivers, and hills. These things are all temporary. They will all, someday, go away.

But the things that really matter—what we are challenged to focus on—are the things that are unseen. God's "eternal glory" (2 Corinthians 4:17) will outshine every single thing—good or bad—that we see on this earth.

So when things get rough, or even when they're great, it helps to remember that there is an unseen reward waiting for you, and for all those who choose to follow God.

Do what I created YOU to do!

MY BOOK SAYS

**Whatever you have learned
or received or heard from me, or seen in me—
put it into practice.
And the God of peace will be with you.**

PHILIPPIANS 4:9

LISTEN REAL CLOSE

Peace doesn't come from doing what everybody wants you to do. It doesn't come from being successful or popular or making everyone happy. True peace comes only from God and from acting in obedience to what you know he wants you to do.

What has God told you about the plans he has for you? What have you learned through reading your Bible and this devotional? What do you hear as you listen and pray?

GET TO IT!

To have a life of true peace, start practicing those things, the things God reveals to you—starting with Philippians 4:9.

Well, what are you waiting for?!
The world is waiting on YOU!

"For I know the plans I have for you," declares the LORD, "plans to prosper you and not to harm you, plans to give you hope and a future."

JEREMIAH 29:11